# THE SOUND OF HIS VOICE

## HE SATISFIES THE LONGING SOUL

# The Sound of His Voice

## HE SATISFIES THE LONGING SOUL

### JEFFREY E. HOFFMAN, MD

# AMBASSADOR INTERNATIONAL
GREENVILLE, SOUTH CAROLINA & BELFAST, NORTHERN IRELAND

www.ambassador-international.com

THE SOUND OF HIS VOICE:
He Satisfies the Longing Soul

©2011 Jeffrey E. Hoffman, MD

Printed in the United States of America

ISBN: 978-1-935507-65-9

Cover Design & Page Layout by Dena Hynes Design: www.creativedena.com

AMBASSADOR INTERNATIONAL
Emerald House
427 Wade Hampton Blvd
Greenville, SC 29609, USA
www.ambassador-international.com

AMBASSADOR BOOKS
The Mount
2 Woodstock Link
Belfast, BT6 8DD, Northern Ireland, UK
www.ambassador-international.com

*The colophon is a trademark of Ambassador*

Patti M. Hummel
President & Agent
The Benchmark Group LLC, Nashville, TN
Pattiq3@aol.com
www.benchmarkgrouppublishers.com

*Dedicated to*

THE BARBER

# Table of Contents

## *Chapter 1:*
### THE MUSIC ON THE MOUNTAIN

Two times in my life I have heard the voice of God, and I am still waiting for the third.

The first occurred when I was five years old. Like most adults, I do not remember much of what happened that long ago, but this memory is crystal clear, as if it happened just yesterday. I was sitting on a tall stool in the doorway of a mountain cabin, looking out over the campground, in the process of having my hair cut.... But I'm getting ahead of myself. You need to know the context surrounding this event if you are to appreciate it as I do.

Sometime before hearing the voice of God the first time, an equally profound event left an indelible mark on my memory. The whole family, all six of us, were going out for dinner to Bob's Big Boy. Bob's Big Boy was a Southern California icon, famous for its burgers, chicken, and other family fare. I am one of four brothers, the second oldest by birth. Much has been made of the effects of birth order on the development of personality, and my personal experience fits with most of it. But that is not part of this story.

All six of us were piled into my father's brand new 1958 Corvette convertible. This was before the days of car seats and child restraint laws. Dad drove, of course, and Mom sat in the passenger seat. Paul, the youngest, sat in front with mom while the rest of us perched on the deck behind the seats. I remember being right behind my father on the left side. It was glorious! The sun was shining, the car rumbled, and the warm Southern California wind blew on our faces. We must have been some sight as we pulled into the parking lot of the restaurant.

I don't remember much about the dinner, but I can still picture the gumball machine that stood by the entrance. Dad was paying the bill at the counter and I asked him for a penny to buy some gum. He obliged and, true to course, my brothers saw what was happening and began asking Dad for a penny of their own. But Dad had already given me his last penny, and that was that. I think Jay, the oldest, still holds it against me that I got the only piece of gum that night. But, little did he know how things would turn out.

I stood eye-level with the slot on the bright red box of the gumball dispenser. There was a silver crank just below it and a glass globe on top, filled with a rainbow of colored gumballs. I slid my penny into the slot, grasped the crank and, hoping for a blue one, gave it a turn. The inner mechanism clinked and rattled as gear worked against gear. I was enchanted. Finally came the plink of the gumball as it landed behind the little silver door. Lifting the door, I saw my prize. It was black, my least favorite. Oh well. I popped it into my mouth as we left the restaurant.

It was a short trip home, but I tired of the gum quickly and began looking around for some way to get rid of it. To this day I don't know what possessed me to do it, but I stuck the gum on the side of Dad's Corvette. I took it out of my mouth, reached over the side, and stuck it right on the shiny red paint! I could have asked for help from Mom or Dad. That would have been the smart thing to do. I could have just thrown it over the side of the car into the street, but I knew that was wrong. Did I know it was also wrong to stick it to the side of the car? Well, yes, but somehow I thought that maybe no one would notice.

They say that innocence is one of the essential qualities of childhood. If this is true then on that day I ceased to be a child. I felt a strange burning sensation somewhere inside as I stuck the gum on the car. It was not pleasant, somewhat akin to nausea. Even with the wind blowing in my face there was a heat growing in my neck and cheeks. What a difference there was between the ride to the restaurant and the ride back home.

By the time we arrived home I was mostly recovered. But the inevitable happened. My father discovered the gum on the side of the car. "Jeffrey," he said, "did you put this gum on the car?"

In an instant the burn returned to my insides, only this time it was much more intense. I had been found out! I panicked and said the first thing that came to my mind. "Jay did it."

I did not know it at the time, but I was replaying one of the oldest scenes in human history. When Adam and Eve took the forbidden fruit, the Bible says, "The eyes of both of them were opened, and they knew that they were naked" (Gen. 3:7 NASB). Have you ever had a dream where you were naked and the people around you were staring? Psychologists say it is a common scenario for dreams. But you don't have to be a psychologist to understand their significance. We all have things about ourselves we want to hide, things about which we are not proud, things which, if found out, would make us feel embarrassed or ashamed. The dream is an expression of our inner fear that our nakedness will be revealed.

Before Adam and Eve ate the forbidden fruit, they had nothing to hide from God, nothing of which to be ashamed, even their naked bodies. Can you imagine the freedom of that feeling? Can you imagine your entire being an open book for all to read and not feeling the least bit embarrassed? Every moment of your history, every thought or desire of your heart, every Internet site you ever accessed? But no one alive could stand that kind of scrutiny. It is lethal, and we will fight to avoid it with every ounce of our strength.

From the moment I stuck the gum on the car I knew I was naked and I hated it. The last thing I wanted was for someone else to discover that I was naked. So I lied and blamed my brother. It was a desperate thing to do, and stupid, but no more stupid than what Adam and Eve did. When God came calling on them after they had eaten the fruit, they tried to hide. How ludicrous a proposition, to hide from God! And when He found them and questioned them, how did they answer? Well, at least they were smart enough not to lie, but they did try to shift the blame. Adam tried to blame Eve for giving him the fruit, and Eve tried to blame the serpent. Both were actually blaming God as well, at least by implication. Adam said, "The woman *whom You gave to be with me,* she gave me from the tree, and I ate" (Gen. 3:12 NASB, emphasis mine). Eve said, "The serpent [one of God's creations] deceived me" (Gen. 3:13 NASB).

God knew the answers to His questions before He asked them, and so did my father. Both were giving the guilty an opportunity to confess. It was the gracious thing to do, but the naked fear exposure more than anything else. The naked do not understand that their condition must be exposed before it can be clothed, and they are foolish enough to think that the truth can be hidden, hidden by a transparent lie or a handful of fig leaves. It is necessary to stand naked before the one you have offended, before the One Who has the power to forgive and cover us up. But it is a terrifying proposition, and it requires a full measure of faith and trust in your forgiver.

When my father asked the question, I was not ready to answer, so I lied and compounded my problems. I have always been amazed at what poor liars children are. Without batting an eye they will offer one logically impossible excuse after another. I was no different. I was the *only* one who had received a penny for gum at the restaurant. I was the only one who had sat on the left side of the car. I was the only one with the opportunity to commit the crime, and I no longer had a piece of gum in my mouth. What was I thinking? Did I really think I could get away with a lie?

I did not get away with it and was sent to my room for punishment. The emotions I experienced after being confronted with the truth may surprise you. Above all else I felt anger. When you think about it, anger is a decidedly inappropriate emotion under those circumstances. Who was I angry with? My father? My brother? What was I angry about? Being punished? Being found out?

As far as I can recall, there was no remorse in my emotions. Maybe a hint of guilt, but not enough to lead to repentance. Can you have guilt without repentance? Sure you can. You can be sorry you were caught, but not sorry for what you did. You can cling to the myth of relative culpability, the smokescreen of environmental stresses, or the outright lie of situational ethics.

But in the end, you knew what you did was wrong and you did it anyway. The only valid emotion is shame. The only valid response is penitence. But we will have none of it. We will fight it at all costs.

But is does cost. It costs us always more than we bargained for. We just fail to see both sides of the equation when we make the bargain. It costs us our most valuable possession, our innocence. And I mean that. What else can you think of that is more valuable to you than your innocence? Without it nothing else in your life is right. You may be happy at times, but you will never experience joy. You may be comfortable at times, but you will never possess peace.

But it does cost us to regain innocence. It costs us our pride. It costs us control. In a way it also costs us freedom, but that is in reality a deception. We just think we are free when we are enslaved to our own guilt. We are enslaved also by the fear of exposing our nakedness, and we have forgotten what real freedom feels like. The typical human response to confrontation with a dangerous truth is anger, anger or denial. It's the classic fight or flight in the face of a threat. We either fight it with anger or we flee from it with denial.

When I was confronted with the truth, my first reaction was flight. I tried to run, metaphorically, from the blame—to put as much distance as possible between me and the truth. And when that didn't work, I switched tactics and shifted into the fight mode. In a split second I shifted from defense to offense. One moment I was running full speed away from this dangerous truth, and the next moment I had turned to face it full on, ready to duke it out.

I think it is amazing that I came up with all this on my own. I had no training or experience in the art of debate. I was just a kid! Yet it all happened so quickly and spontaneously, bursting forth with all the appearance of a well-thought-out plan. The parents I meet in my practice often share with me their own amazement at similar behaviors in their children. Well, perhaps "amazement" is not the right word. Something more like "surprise" and "irritation" maybe.

So, who teaches a child these things? Who teaches him how to lie and defy his parents? And where does the anger and rage come from? Is it instinct, survival of the fittest? Some would argue that is all it is, and that all behavior is simply the result of various causes and effects. And, for the most part, I don't disagree with this explanation, except that it leaves out one of the most important causes of all—God.

I was angry with my parents, and by extension, and more fundamentally, I was angry with God. Being angry with your accuser is a defense mechanism designed to protect you from the reality of the situation. When your mind is preoccupied with anger, it doesn't have time to think about the truth. But like many defense mechanisms, anger is ultimately self-destructive. It eats away, almost literally, at your soul, and only the truth can set you free.

Psalm 2:1 (KJV) asks the rhetorical question, "Why do the heathen rage, and the people imagine a vain thing?" the answer being, "Because they are crazy!" The God of the universe (or your parents if you are a child) is the absolute and all-powerful authority over everything, and it is just plain crazy to be angry with Him about anything. But fortunately for us, God is very patient, and He understands our emotions. After all, He made us creatures of emotion. He also gave us intelligence and a will, and He expects us to use all our parts so that we will eventually come to our senses.

In that moment of defiance, as a five-year-old child, I was confronted with one of the most devastating truths a human can know. I was confronted with the fact that I was a sinner. And I quickly learned that one of the primary consequences of sin is broken relationships. My parents were not happy with me, and I was angry with them. But I didn't care; at least that's what I told myself. Even though a simple confession would have resolved the matter, I wanted nothing to do with it. So I clung to my anger, hoping to find in it the strength to resist reason.

I entertained this insanity until the day I sat on the barber's stool. I'm not sure how long a time that was, but my father, in his wisdom, judged it had been long enough. Both he and my mother recognized my anxiety. My mother says she could see it in my eyes. So as my father cut my hair, he shared with me a remedy for my dilemma. He did not address my anger; that was just a distraction. He did not remind me of my sins; he knew they were all too obvious to me. He told me, simply, that if I wanted to be forgiven all I had to do was ask. "Ask and you shall receive," is what Jesus said. Ask forgiveness of the God you have offended and He *will* forgive you. The hardest part is admitting that you need forgiveness. It exposes your nakedness. It is a massively risky undertaking, and it hurts like crazy. No one can deny it, and no one should soft-pedal the cost. But in the end it really doesn't cost you anything of value. It's just hard to see it at the time.

Right there on that barber's stool I asked God to forgive me, and I heard His voice. It sounded like music. It was a melody, rather than words, and it spoke peace to my heart. The world outside the door of the cabin seemed to brighten. I had not realized how dark it had been. The air now felt warm and sweet. I had not realized how cold and bitter it had been. I got down off the stool and walked outside. I felt lighter than air. I had not realized how heavy was the burden I had been carrying.

Part of what I heard was what some have called the music of the spheres. The universe, which God created, is constantly speaking to those who have ears to hear. It is giving continuous testimony to the glorious nature of its Creator. Part of what I heard was the celebration that was taking place in heaven over the salvation of another soul. But part of what I heard was God Himself expressing His uncontained pleasure with me. His pleasure with *me!* Disgraceful, naked, rotten, little old me. But He didn't see me that way anymore, and I knew it. He saw me as beautiful and fully clothed. I didn't understand it at the time, but in truth He saw me fully clothed in the righteousness of His Son.

The first time I heard God's voice, He answered my question, **"Who am I?"** He answered by saying, **"You are my beloved."**

The sound of that music still rings in my ears.

## *Chapter 2:*
### THE LIGHT IN THE JUNGLE

The second time I heard the voice of God I was in the jungles of Guatemala.

It was the summer of my seventeenth year. I was doing mission work with the Friends Church, helping to relocate families from an impoverished, overpopulated part of the country to a virgin jungle. The soil there was rich and the water was clean. Families could easily grow more than enough food to sustain themselves. They could also raise extra cash crops of rice and bananas. One of my jobs was driving them to the market twice a week where they could sell their crops and buy other goods with the profits.

I was living with a missionary family from the States who had devoted their lives to this work. They were the most generous and loving people I have ever met. The hardships they suffered were never counted, but I saw them. When Virginia lost a diaper pin, there was no extra to replace it, not until the next trip to the market. Ray had to make do with one Coke a day, and there was no root beer. A small thing, you might think, but not if root beer is your favorite. If the truck broke down, you were through. Repair parts could take weeks to arrive.

The house we lived in was genuinely primitive. The walls were all single sheets of plywood with no insulation. Rafters and eaves were open to enhance ventilation. When it rained, which it did every day that time of year, the tin roof thundered, sometimes so loudly you couldn't carry on a conversation. I've always loved the sound of rain falling on a roof. Perhaps that's because it rained so rarely in semi-arid Southern California where I grew up.

One day, Ray took me exploring the undeveloped parcels of land that were part of the relocation project. The jungle was thickest there with some of the old growth timber still standing. He showed me how to cut a section of water vine and take a drink. It tasted like cinnamon. We also took turns swinging from huge vines, just like Tarzan. I even jumped into the small jungle river and swam for a while against the current. It was a teenager's paradise! The only drawback was that later that night I developed a nasty case of hives. Apparently I'm allergic to the water vine. Too bad. I sure would like to taste it again someday.

One night I was alone in my room reading my Bible. The generator was still running and the light from the single bulb hanging from the rafters was more than enough for my young eyes. I was reading 1 John, chapter 1. I read it through several times and kept returning to part of verse 5: "God is light, and in him is no darkness at all"

(KJV). The words just seemed to sit on the page. I felt like they should mean something more to me. I got down on my knees and prayed, "God, show me what this means." I continued to pray and reread the words until I sensed something in the room. It was not a startling sense like the movement of a snake or a wild animal. That had happened to me all too often since coming to the jungles of Guatemala. It was why you always carried a machete with you wherever you went.

The something I sensed appeared as a light in the corner of the room. But it was more than a light; it was a familiar Presence. Gradually, the intensity of light and the sense of Presence increased. In that moment I knew I was in the presence of God. I averted my eyes. It only seemed right to do so. God was showing Himself to me, giving me a glimpse into His true nature, giving me a gift of unparalleled value.

Although there was nothing threatening about the Presence, there was an unquestionable aura of absolute authority and power. And though I have used the word "light" to describe what I saw, I must confess that that word is not quite right. It does not do it justice. The light I saw was something more than ordinary light. It seemed to bend and fill all the shadows in the room. It was alive, penetrating, and pure. Yes, "pure" is the best word to describe it. "God is light, and in him is no darkness at all." This was pure light, and it was breathtaking.

In the Bible, there are only three "divine equations": God is love, God is light, and God is spirit. By contrast, there are any number of verses that describe God. The descriptive verses teach us about God's character and personality. The equations define His nature.

What do we know about God's character and personality? We know that God is good, continually seeking the welfare of His creation. We know that God is holy, separate from all that is impure. We know that He is righteous, upholding the moral order of the universe. We know that He has certain incommunicable attributes such as omnipotence, omniscience, and immutability. We know that God can be merciful and forgiving, but we also know He can be angry and jealous. God is all these together at the same time.

But how are we to understand the divine equations? I believe that each divine equation, properly understood, is a complete description of the nature of God.

Think for a minute about what it means that God is love. The way that God loves us, in truth, tells us everything about His personality. God's love is sweet, tender, forgiving, gracious, and merciful *and* it is tough, unrelenting, uncompromising, powerful, and limitless. God showed His love for that little five-year-old child who stuck his gum on the side of the car by offering His own Son to pay the penalty for his sin. His love for that child was sweet, tender, forgiving, gracious, and merciful, *and* it was tough, unrelenting, uncompromising, powerful, and limitless. You see, God cannot help but notice the gum on the door. He knows it must be dealt with if the heart of the child is to be healed. He knows it must be dealt with if the relationship is to be restored. This principle is captured in one of the most familiar verses in

Scripture, John 3:16: "For God so loved the world, that He gave His only begotten Son, that whoever believes in Him shall not perish, but have eternal life" (NASB).

This was the music I heard on that barber stool on the mountain. The music taught me that God is love. And if the music I heard on the barber stool taught me that God is love, then the Presence in the jungle showed me that God is light. The meaning of this second divine equation is perhaps less obvious than the first. Everyone thinks they understand what it means that God is love, even if their understanding is incomplete. But what does it mean that God is light? To understand this better, let me return now to where I left off in the jungle.

As the light began to grow in the room, I remember looking around and noticing that it seemed to cast no shadows anywhere. It was as if the light passed through the solid objects in the room, or bent around them, until it had filled every space; every space, that is, except for one dark smudge in the center of my chest. As you might imagine, I found this rather alarming. What was this dark smudge doing in the center of my chest? Why had the light not penetrated it? And, what was the light going to think about it? Then, the verse echoed again more loudly in my mind: "God is light, and in him is no darkness at all."

Until that day I had always thought of myself as a relatively good person. And I suppose I was. I never willfully disobeyed my parents. I worked hard in school and was generous with my friends. I never did go through an adolescent period of rebellion.

But compared to the light, my heart was as black as coal. The Light revealed this darkness in me.

Ordinarily, light eliminates darkness. When you flip on a switch, the darkness in a room disappears. But this light was different. This light revealed the darkness in my heart. And I think this is very meaningful. The light of God may be supernaturally powerful, able to penetrate and bend where ordinary light cannot, but it has certain self-imposed limits. Self-imposed by God Himself.

Because God created man with free will, He allows man to limit the extent of His light. Man can choose to block God's light from penetrating his heart. This concept is explained by John in his Gospel:

"This is the judgment, that the Light has come into the world, and men loved the darkness rather than the Light, for their deeds were evil. For everyone who does evil hates the Light, and does not come to the Light for fear that his deeds will be exposed" (3:19–20 NASB).

That night in the jungle I chose to "come to the light." I suppose it would be more accurate to say I invited the light to come closer to me, but the effect was the same. I saw the light of God and gained a fuller appreciation of His true nature. At the same time I became aware of the contrast between the light of God and the darkness that remained in my heart. It was not as if God was pointing His finger at me and saying, "Look at that darkness in your heart! You should be ashamed!" It was nothing like that at all.

What He did was show me more of Himself. What he did was say, "Look at me." And when I did, everything became clear.

In the Bible, we are warned against comparing ourselves with those around us. Those comparisons lead to either pride or discouragement, and God does not want us to go in either of those directions. But when we look at God, we are bound to notice that we are less than Him. We are bound to sense that there is yet a part of us that He cannot tolerate, a part that is limiting our relationship with Him.

And God is so amazing. Though He is offended by our sin, He never focuses on it. And He does not want us to focus on it either. He has the ability to imagine what we would look like without sin, and that's what He loves, and that's what He will make sure that we become.

The second time I heard the voice of God, he answered my question, **"Who are You?"** He answered by saying, **"I am the One Who is holy."**

Ever since that day I have been searching the Scriptures, searching for and finding more and more of His light.

## *Chapter 3:*
## THE WARMTH OF HIS PRESENCE

I opened my first medical practice in a small town in rural Oregon. I was right out of residency, young, just twenty-eight years old, and painfully naïve, and overnight I was all alone running a solo practice in pediatrics. My education and training had been good. Well, good enough, anyway. You see, mostly what you learn in medical school and residency is how to save lives. You don't really learn how to practice medicine, and you certainly don't learn how to deal with local medical politics. Regarding the latter, it would be no exaggeration to say that I was in for a real trial by fire. But, here again I am getting ahead of myself.

I was a senior in high school before I decided what I wanted to do with my life. I was smart, and I knew it. Smart enough, I was told, to pursue any career or profession I wanted. I just didn't know what that might be. I had a certain aptitude for languages, and my mother thought I should consider becoming a Wycliffe Bible translator. However, my heart was more drawn to the life sciences and medicine in particular. My parents arranged for me to take a series of psychological tests to help me answer the question. The tests were designed to determine a person's abilities and interests and then, based on those results, recommend a suitable career. Of course I prayed about this regularly. But no answer seemed to come from that source.

I remember at the conclusion of the tests and after reviewing the results, the psychologist simply asked me, "Well, Jeff, what do you want to do?" I answered, "I think I'd like to be a doctor." His response to my answer was completely noncommittal. "You could do that, if you want to." And that was that. I was really expecting him to tell me what I *should* do. But he didn't. I felt like saying, "I thought *you* were supposed to answer that question." But I couldn't say that. It just wasn't in my nature to be so assertive.

I continued to pray, but there was no music and no light. There was no word from the Lord. So I tried to reason my way through to a decision. I weighed the pros and cons, but what does a seventeen-year-old really know about the pros and cons of being a physician? In the end, because I felt that being a doctor was a high calling in life and I apparently had the ability to become one, I decided this was what I *should* do. It troubled me that God had not been more overt with His leading in such an important decision, but I trusted that if He really had some other plan in mind for me He would make it known.

After high school, I began my pre-med courses in college. In truth, I did not have a back-up plan. This is something I certainly would not advise for anyone else in my situation. Only a very small percentage of "pre-med" freshman college students ever make it all the way into medical school. Even those who make the grade in college still face very stiff competition for the limited number of slots available in the freshman medical classes. I really have no idea what I would have done if I had not been accepted to medical school as a senior in college. But I was accepted, and my life continued on its determined course.

But was this the course that God wanted me to take? Does the fact that I made it into medical school prove that this was God's plan for my life? Well, no. Though the odds were stacked against me, one should never trust the odds to determine God's will. And what if God seems to be blessing your life, opening doors, and paving the way? Is that an indication that you are doing His will? Well, no. I imagine God is comfortable blessing us over a fairly broad range of life choices. What we really want to know is if we are at the center of His will, if we are following His highest and best plan for our lives. But how can we know that for sure?

---

The decision to propose to my wife was another one that caused me years of turmoil. As far back as I can remember I always felt I was destined to marry. I knew I needed intimacy beyond friendship, and, oddly enough, this sort of frightened me. I did not like the thought of needing someone else, and I was afraid God might not appreciate it. Imagine that. The God Who had created me and chosen me, the God Who knew me intimately and only wanted the best for me, *that* God might not appreciate the deepest needs of my heart? I remember times of complete and tearful surrender when I gave everything over to God. But I also remember times of holding back, fearful times when I did not want to trust God with this matter.

You see, I had been in love with Marcy, my future spouse, since junior high school. Sure, there were other girls along the way, but none of them held a candle to her. I wanted her, and I was afraid that God might not see it my way. I suppose at the root of my dilemma was this question: Did I love God more than Marcy? To put it another way, did I love myself, my desires, my life more than I loved Him? I was wrestling with Jesus' words, "He that loveth his life shall lose it; and he that hateth his life in this world shall keep it unto life eternal" (John 12:25 KJV).

And Jesus was asking me the same question He had asked Peter: "Jeff, son of Walt, do you love me more than these?"

In truth, my answer to His question was no more certain than Peter's. Yes, I was sure I loved Him. I was sure I wanted to love Him more than anything else, but I wasn't sure I did. Fortunately, that was good enough for Him.

In the end, God did not tell me in any overt way that I should marry Marcy. Perhaps I wasn't listening, or perhaps, as I have said, I was afraid to hear what He might say. But in the end, I decided it was the right thing to do, and the rightness of that decision has been proven over again countless times since.

Not that our marriage has at all times been one long bed of roses. I had tons to learn about relationships and about how to treat the woman you love. One of the more telling lessons came on the day I proposed. To my surprise, Marcy said she wanted to think about it. Unbelievable! I'd been thinking about it for over eight years. What had she been doing all this time? Didn't she know that this was obviously the right thing to do? In this I was incredibly naïve. I did not understand how vital it was for us to have a conversation about the future. Even God has been known to carry on a conversation with Himself. (In the first chapter of the Bible, God says, "Let *Us* make man in Our image…" [Gen. 1:26 NASB, emphasis mine]. And again in the third chapter, God says, "Behold, the man has become like one of *Us,* knowing good and evil…" [Gen. 3:22 NASB, emphasis mine].) I, on the other hand, am such an extreme introvert that this essential requirement of human relationships was beyond me. But, God bless her, Marcy tolerated my little fit over the delay in her decision and decided to marry me anyway. She had known me for almost a decade. She knew what she was getting into, well, mostly, and she chose me anyway. That was grace at work. Thank God!

---

Returning to the story of my first practice, I have to say that at that time I was blindsided by the world. I had no idea how self-serving, bitter, and down-right evil people could be. It was a combination of things that had left me unprepared for this challenge. First was the fact that I'd been "blessed" with a fairly sheltered life. I suppose nothing truly bad had ever happened to me. I'd suffered no major setbacks in my life. Also, I had a natural tendency to always believe the best of people even when the facts argued otherwise. Perhaps I thought it was the "Christian" thing to do. But it was naïve and unrealistic. Since those early years I have grown to appreciate Jesus' advice to be "wise as serpents and innocent as doves" (Matt. 10:16 ESV).

For the most part, the problems I encountered in my first practice were not personal. No one was really out to get me, well, with maybe one exception, but we don't need to go into that at this time. The real problem was that I had landed right in the middle of a hornet's nest. Various factions of the medical community and the local hospital administration had pitted themselves against each other in a feud that had been going on for years. One group of surgeons was trying to develop a free-standing surgical center apart from the hospital, and of course the hospital administration did not like that. The other surgeons aligned themselves with the hospital and would have nothing to do with the "surgi-center" surgeons. The internists in town refused to share "call" with each other, which is a customary relationship between doctors allowing them time off from their practices. Without such arrangements a doctor has to be available to his patients 24/7/365. The family practitioners, who had been used to ruling the roost for decades, resented the arrival of specialists, specialists like myself, a pediatrician. Rules were passed in committees that adversely affected one group over another, and somehow, no matter what I said or did, I was always caught in the middle. It was an absolute nightmare.

In my unvarnished innocence, all I thought I would have to do is hang out my shingle, be nice, and play fair. The population was large enough to support two or three pediatricians, and the other issues seemed to be largely between other doctors on the staff. I just wanted to get along and offer my services to the community.

Why, you may ask, did I ever think to move into this hornet's nest? The truth is I did not know how bad it was at the time. But there were other factors that blinded me to the facts even as they became increasingly apparent.

You see, some time before the move, my brothers and I, along with my parents, decided we would all like to live together in the same small town in the Northwest. We had grown up in Southern California and watched it change from a series of quiet suburbs into a hectic, overcrowded parking lot (no offense to those who do like living there). We also shared a common faith and heritage and wanted our children to grow up together with all their cousins. It was a grand scheme, and this small town in central Oregon looked like our best hope for pulling it off. Surely this dream was a good thing. Surely it was the kind of dream that God would bless, a dream that honored family, faith, and traditional values. But was it God's will? Was there any way to be certain? Were we just to step out in faith and see what happened? Lacking a bolt out of the blue or a fleece in the night, what else could we do? We had to move somewhere, and anyway, if this was not the place, then surely God would intervene and show us otherwise, right?

So, I landed in the hornet's nest and suffered there for twelve years. Much of that suffering Marcy and I kept to ourselves. We were there, after all, for the good of our children and our extended family. In truth, much good did come of it anyway. To this day my children and their cousins look back on those years with great fondness. All of them are following the Lord, to greater or lesser degrees. My children married native Oregonians who are truly awesome, making me one of the luckiest father-in-laws on the planet. My son even became a physician himself! So life was good, just hard, and very hard at times.

I prayed often that God might send me a medical partner to share call and ease my burden. For one whole year I fasted once a week and devoted extra hours to prayer, but no answer came. No music, no light, no voice of any kind that I could detect, until the twelfth year when Marcy and I really began to feel that we couldn't take it any longer. In desperation, we finally asked God the "forbidden" question: "God, do you want us to move?" Asking it meant admitting failure and abandoning our dream. It even implied that God had possibly failed us.

I cannot tell you the sense of relief we felt once we honestly allowed ourselves to ask that question. Clarity came almost overnight, and within thirty days I had closed my practice and moved to a more pediatrician-friendly community. In the end we did not feel that we had failed or that God had failed us after all. The community had failed us and God simply had a different and better plan for our lives.

---

In all these decisions, and many others, I had sought God's "perfect will" for my life. Do you know what I mean by that? Let me explain. There is a theory, or belief, that God has an ideal or "perfect" plan for each of our lives. Following that plan will result in two things: maximum glory to God and maximum joy and fulfillment for us. It is a win-win situation with eternal rewards. Now, even the most stalwart of believers in this theory knows that nobody ever follows that plan to the letter. Not Moses, David, Elijah, or even Mother Theresa. This means the "perfect plan" is always in flux. Whenever we fail to make the perfect decision, which may be nearly all the time, the plan must of necessity change to accommodate that wrong decision. Our 'GPS route' is constantly being 'recalculated' so that in practice the perfect will of God is a complex matter.

On the other hand, the fundamental principles behind it are quite simple. Because God loves us, because He knows what is best for us (He *is* omniscient), and because He is continually involved in our lives, working for the best possible outcome, there must, therefore, be a perfect will of God for our lives. If this is true, then it is only reasonable to want God's will for our lives. In fact, it would be ridiculous to want anything else.

I suspect my experiences in seeking God's will for the decisions in my life are not unlike those of most believers. We know that the Bible is full of promises for divine guidance. Jesus was very specific with His disciples in promising guidance through the Holy Spirit. We also know that there are countless examples in Scripture of God's providing that guidance to real flesh-and-blood people. But, for many of us, we feel our experience with that guidance falls short. We may read biographies of famous Christians or hear spectacular testimonies in church, but these, at least in part, can discourage rather than inspire. If God did it for them, why doesn't He do it for me?

And, I suppose I am better off than many believers. At least in my case, I could look back on two occasions when I did hear the voice of God. I could say I knew from experience that God can and will speak when He wants to. So then, why did God seem silent when it came to the decisions and choices of my life? What might be the problem?

I have learned over the years that problems in our relationship with God may be caused by one of three things: sin, spiritual immaturity, and personality. I don't think I've ever seen it explained this way before, so let me elaborate.

First, and obviously, sin in our lives can block the blessing of God. It usually starts as a particular sin blocking a particular blessing, but it doesn't stop there. Spiritual immaturity is either natural, due to youth and inexperience, or self-induced, due to resistance to training. Finally, individual personality and natural strengths and weaknesses will impact our relationship with God just as they impact everything else in our lives. It should be understood, at least in my opinion, that personalities are not entirely fixed things. We do change over time, at least to some degree, through life experiences, through self-reflection, and in relationships with other people and with God. Fortunately, God is aware of all these things and is constantly at work in our lives to help get the best out of us.

On the other hand, what if there really was no problem and things were happening exactly as God intended them? What if I had been looking at this whole thing the wrong way? To put it another way, what if I had been listening for God's voice with the wrong ears? You know, when God spoke to me on the mountain, I heard music, and when He spoke to me in the jungle, I saw light; but now He was trying to speak to me in a third way. And when it came to this third way, was I naturally or spiritually hard of hearing?

---

Regarding personality and natural strengths and weaknesses, by now the reader may already have a pretty good idea about what mine might be. According to the Myers-Briggs personality inventory (a paper and pencil test that helps one learn about their own personality type), I am an "INTJ," which means I am basically an introvert who evaluates information intuitively (rather than experientially), who makes decisions based on logic and thinking rather than feeling, and who prefers a consistent and organized environment. According to the Enneagram, another personality inventory, I am an "investigator," which is characterized as intense, cerebral, perceptive, innovative, secretive, and isolated.

And, you know, there's nothing wrong with any of that. I am who God made me. I have certain natural abilities and disabilities, certain strengths and weaknesses. In that regard, I am no better or worse than anyone else.

These systems of personality analysis, the Myers-Briggs and the Enneagram, are rather complicated. Most people have not found the time or opportunity to complete one. So I would like to suggest a much simpler way of learning about yourself that requires only an understanding of your preferred "learning style." In truth, this version has not been subjected to as much scientific study as the others, but many do find it helpful, as I have. It goes as follows.

It has been said that humans learn in one of three basic ways: through our eyes (visual input), through our ears (auditory input), or through experience (hands-on practice). We each have a preferred method of learning, making us visual, auditory, or experiential learners, by preference. Let me explain.

The auditory learner can listen to a lecture in class and remember most of what is said. For the visual learner, the words of the lecture seem to go in one ear and out the other, and it is not until he or she is home reading over the lecture notes that he or she is able to grasp the subject. The experiential learner doesn't get much out of either hearing the lecture or reading the notes. It is not until he or she is in the laboratory running the experiment or applying the concepts that this type of learner finally understands. The experiential learner must see, hear, smell, feel, and experience the process in order to understand the concept.

In my medical practice, I have found understanding learning styles to be helpful in working with parents. Some of my parents learn best through conversation and dialogue. Some benefit most from a written note, a handout, or a suggested reading. Others need me to demonstrate my meaning, especially when it involves a procedure or dosing schedule for a medicine. People who favor this last learning type benefit from stories of how the intervention has worked out in my own life or the lives of my other patients. What all these parents have in common is the need to be taught in a truly effective way.

Now the point I'm trying to make here is a really big one. When God speaks to us, He undoubtedly takes into account the unique nature of our personality—what our own preferences and proclivities are, and how we think and learn. And if my understanding is correct, then there are three basic ways He has for doing this. He can speak to our hearts in conversation, He can speak to our minds in revelation, and He can speak to our spirits in relationship. As you might have guessed, I can relate best to revelation, to visual and written communication. But like all people, I need all that God can give me—all the information and all the help in all ways I can possibly receive them. I must not settle for the voice I find easiest or most natural to hear. I must not settle for His meeting the needs that only *I* perceive.

When God spoke to me on the barber chair, I heard music, and it ministered to my heart. It was the voice of the Father, the God Who is love, telling me that I am His beloved. When He spoke to me in the jungle, I saw light, and my mind gained unprecedented understanding. That was the voice of the Son, the God Who is light, telling me Who it is Who loves me. Today, I am still trying to tune my ears to hear the third voice of God, but I suspect this third way probably feels like a touch. It probably feels like the light touch of a hand on the shoulder, or the warmth of another body standing close by, or possibly, at times, as much as a full embrace. I suspect that voice is heard best not with our minds, and not even with our hearts, but with that other mysterious part of ourselves known as the spirit. And if the spirit is anything, it is the part of our being that enables us to have a relationship with God. The third voice of God, then, would be the voice of the Spirit, of the God Who is spirit; the One Who comes alongside us to comfort us, guide us, teach us, and minister peace to our souls. For me, this third voice is the most subtle of the three, and I believe there are more reasons for this than just my personality.

---

It was hard telling my extended family that Marcy and I and our children were leaving our small town where my brothers and parents had settled together. They had all made sacrifices to share the dream of raising our children together in the same town. I was afraid they might feel betrayed or abandoned. But they didn't. As it turned out, they understood what I had been going through and were more aware of my pain than I had realized. They were deeply sad, and it was very difficult, but, in the end, they knew it was the right thing to do.

My youngest brother, Paul, was the most hurt by the loss. I remember crying together with him and wondering out loud why our plans had not worked out. Had we been wrong in thinking that we had been following God's will for our lives? Why did it appear that God had withdrawn His blessing? Together, we turned for comfort to Jesus' words in John 14–16. In that passage, Jesus is telling His disciples that He will be leaving them soon and the "Comforter" will be sent to them to meet their ongoing needs:

> ...I will pray the Father, and he shall give you another Comforter, that he may abide with you for ever; even the Spirit of truth.... These things have I spoken unto you, being yet present with you. But the Comforter, which is the Holy

Ghost, whom the Father will send in my name, he shall teach you all things, and bring all things to your remembrance, whatsoever I have said unto you. Peace I leave with you, my peace I give unto you: not as the world giveth, give I unto you. Let not your heart be troubled, neither let it be afraid. ... But because I have said these things unto you, sorrow hath filled your heart. Nevertheless I tell you the truth; It is expedient for you that I go away: for if I go not away, the Comforter will not come unto you; but if I depart, I will send him unto you. ... These things I have spoken unto you, that in me ye might have peace. In the world ye shall have tribulation: but be of good cheer; I have overcome the world (John 14:16–17, 25–27; 16:6–7, 33 KJV).

First, let me make one point very clear. There is no sense in which my leaving the small town in Oregon is analogous to Jesus' leaving His disciples to go to the Father. That is not my point at all. My point has to do with the role of the Spirit in our lives.

While Jesus was present on earth, He was God in the flesh, the complete representation of all God is. When He left the earth, He sent the Spirit, Whom He called the "Comforter," to take over that role. The Spirit, now, is the presence of God on earth and in our lives. According to this passage, we are meant to experience God now through His spirit. It is the Spirit Who comes alongside us to comfort us, guide us, teach us, and speak peace to our souls.

The Father has a contrasting role. He is the One to Whom we pray. He is the One Who answers our prayers. He is, by this way of understanding, the One with Whom we have a conversation. And His half of the conversation always speaks to us words of love.

The Son also has a role that contrasts with that of the Spirit and the Father. The Son is the Light of the World, the Word become flesh so that we could see it with our own eyes. He is the visible representation of the Father. He is revelation incarnate.

Now, it is important to keep in mind that God is *all* these at the same time and all in perfect balance. We humans, by contrast, tend to be unbalanced. We tend to be more or less visual, auditory, or experiential in our learning styles, and we tend to relate better to one aspect of the Trinity over the others. We also tend to have a greater or lesser need for words of love, revelation of truth, or a comforting touch. In my case, I only needed to learn once as a child that God loves me, and I have never doubted it since. I only needed to see once what it means that God is light, and I find myself most drawn to this aspect of His nature because it is a reflection of my own. The area where I seem to have the greatest need and the most difficulty is in my relationship with the Spirit.

---

One of the most dramatic stories in the entire Bible is recorded in Luke, chapter 24. It takes place on the road from Jerusalem to the village of Emmaus, three day after Jesus' crucifixion. Please take a few moments to read it through:

That same day two of Jesus' followers were walking to the village of Emmaus, seven miles from Jerusalem. As they walked along they were talking about everything that had happened. As they talked and discussed these things, Jesus himself suddenly came and began walking with them. But God kept them from recognizing him.

He asked them, "What are you discussing so intently as you walk along?"

They stopped short, sadness written across their faces. Then one of them, Cleopas, replied, "You must be the only person in Jerusalem who hasn't heard about all the things that have happened there the last few days."

"What things?" Jesus asked.

"The things that happened to Jesus, the man from Nazareth," they said. "He was a prophet who did powerful miracles, and he was a mighty teacher in the eyes of God and all the people. But our leading priests and other religious leaders handed him over to be condemned to death, and they crucified him. We had hoped he was the Messiah who had come to rescue Israel. This all happened three days ago. Then some women from our group of his followers were at his tomb early this morning, and they came back with an amazing report. They said his body was missing, and they had seen angels who told them Jesus is alive! Some of our men ran out to see, and sure enough, his body was gone, just as the women had said."

Then Jesus said to them, "You foolish people! You find it so hard to believe all that the prophets wrote in the Scriptures. Wasn't it clearly predicted that the Messiah would have to suffer all these things before entering his glory?" Then Jesus took them through the writings of Moses and all the prophets, explaining from all the Scriptures the things concerning himself.

By this time they were nearing Emmaus and the end of their journey. Jesus acted as if he were going on, but they begged him, "Stay the night with us, since it is getting late." So he went home with them. As they sat down to eat, he took the bread and blessed it. Then he broke it and gave it to them. Suddenly, their eyes were opened, and they recognized him. And at that moment he disappeared!

They said to each other, "Didn't our hearts burn within us as he talked with us on the road and explained the Scriptures to us?" And within the hour they were on their way back to Jerusalem. There they found the eleven disciples and the others who had gathered with them, who said, "The Lord has really risen! He appeared to Peter" (Luke 24:13–32 NLT).

I have often imagined myself being there on the road to Emmaus, walking with Jesus and the two followers, listening to Jesus teaching from the Scriptures. It is for me, more or less, an exercise in meditation. But there is a real sense in which all believers are travelers on the road to Emmaus. All of us live in the time between His crucifixion and His full manifestation to the world as the resurrected Lord. We all live in a time of uncertainty, a time of doubt and even despair. We all live in a time when the presence of God on earth and in our lives is veiled. And this is deliberate, I believe, in order that our faith may grow.

You see, faith is *the* essential ingredient in a relationship with God. The author of Hebrews says that "without faith it is impossible to please [God]" (11:6 KJV), and he defines faith as "the substance of things hoped for, the evidence of things not seen" (11:1 KJV).

When you think about it, an audible voice or a supernatural sign pretty much removes the need for faith. These things that you can see and hear cannot be denied. But there is something special and important about learning to trust God when things are not so obvious, to trust Him when it has been a long time since you heard His voice, to trust Him when the current facts seem to be stacking up against Him.

On the road to Emmaus, Jesus' identity was deliberately hidden from the travelers, but not entirely. After He had broken the bread and the truth was revealed, the travelers spoke of an inner sense that there was something special about this stranger. They said their "hearts [burned] within" them. What was it, do you think, that they sensed? Was it not the presence of God, deeply veiled, at their sides? Were they not, in fact, hearing the third voice of God? The voice that comes alongside, the voice that comforts, guides, teaches, and speaks peace to the troubled heart? The voice that is sensed as the warmth of a body standing close by, the gentle touch of a hand on the shoulder, or the caress of a loving embrace?

If the presence of God with us is His third voice, then with that voice God answers our question, **"Where are you?"** He answers by saying, **"I am right here beside you."**

Each day, and for the rest of my life, I will seek to better hear that voice and to understand why that voice is the hardest for me to hear.

## Chapter 4:
## THE TROUBLED HEART

The barber stool I spoke of in the first chapter of this narrative stood in the doorway of a cabin at a Christian camp called Quaker Meadow. I practically grew up at that camp. My parents served often as camp directors, speakers, and counselors and they brought my brothers and me along even before we were old enough to attend camp on our own. Certainly most of the highlights of my spiritual life occurred there in the mountains of the High Sierras of California.

Quaker Meadow had hiking trails, a lake, a swimming pool, spectacular mountain vistas, and, most thrilling to me of all, giant old growth redwoods. Their scientific name is Sequoia gigantium, the largest single living thing on earth.* One cannot begin to

---

*With the possible exception of the peat bogs of Scotland, the quaking aspen of the Rockies, and the Great Barrier Reef, but that depends on how you define "single living thing."

describe the overwhelming sense of awe as you stand at the base of one of these colossal giants. All one's senses are assaulted at the same time. The soft, rich mulch gives gently as you walk up to the trunk. There is a fresh smell that is both warm and earthy. If you stand close, the red, rough bark of the trunk completely fills your peripheral vision. High above the branches, patches of bright blue sky peek through, occasionally marked by a tiny black dot of a passing bird. And when you look around you notice the filtered light sparkling on dust particles floating in the air.

One of the oldest trees in that section of the forest in the camp had been given the name "King David." It was estimated to be about as old as that great monarch of Israel. It was hard to imagine that gigantic living thing as a mere seedling, but like all living things it had had a small and humble beginning. Why had it survived where countless of its siblings had not? Had God intervened? Well, probably not. It had survived simply because of the natural order of things, the way God had created them. And here it had stood for almost 3,000 years.

Every trip to Quaker Meadow I made sure to visit King David. Somehow that tree stood for all the things that camp meant for me. As soon as I was able I would make the half-hour hike down the trail to say hello to my old friend. I would smell the air and run my hand over the tree's bark. Sometimes I would lie down on the soft mulch and watch wispy clouds drift by far above its highest branches. I often wondered if the Garden of Eden had looked something like this. I often hoped, if God would allow it, that I could live in a part of heaven that looked like this part of the forest.

———————————————————

In the winter of 2002 record-breaking storms blew through the High Sierras of California, and King David fell. After standing upright for some 3,000 years, it now lay on its side, decomposing on the forest floor. Can you imagine the thundering crash it made when it fell? Perhaps the sound was muffled somewhat by the snow, but still it is hard to imagine. And of course, anything and everything that lay in its path was obliterated, smashed to smithereens.

True, King David was just a tree. It had lived to a ripe old age, even for a Sequoia gigantium. But, as I said, this tree represented a lot to me. When I heard the news of its fall, I felt a deep loss, an empty sadness. I found pictures of the uprooted tree on the Internet, and they were more disturbing to me than an open casket at a funeral. I tried to be logical about it, but I couldn't help how I felt. It just couldn't be true. King David had been there for thousands of years. My life, by contrast, was no more than a blip on its radar, a mere inch on its yards of growth rings. King David was supposed to be there long after I was gone. How could I have lived to see it fall?

I suppose the loss of King David made me feel like I had lost a part of my childhood. I could no longer be the child who lay at its feet watching the clouds passing by high above its branches. I have always been prone to melancholy, and even little things can trigger it, and this was a big one.

They say that the death of a parent has a certain unique impact on the children who are left behind. As long as a parent lives, a child can still fill the role of a child. As long as a parent lives, even an adult child can feel relatively immortal. But when a parent dies, the child becomes the elder, and nothing remains standing between the child and the grave. The pretense is over. The vulnerability of everything in this life can no longer be denied. The passing of this ancient tree somehow had a similar effect on me.

When King David fell, I was forced to face this reality. Life and death are inevitable. Childhood ends, life moves on, and all things change. And we may live to see the end of great and wondrous things. This reality is expressed poetically by the author of Ecclesiastes:

There is a time for everything, and a season for every activity under the heavens: a time to be born and a time to die, a time to plant and a time to uproot, a time to kill and a time to heal, a time to tear down and a time to build, a time to weep and a time to laugh, a time to mourn and a time to dance, a time to scatter stones and a time to gather them, a time to embrace and a time to refrain from embracing, a time to search and a time to give up, a time to keep and a time to throw away, a time to tear and a time to mend, a time to be silent and a time to speak, a time to love and a time to hate, a time for war and a time for peace. … [God] has made everything beautiful in its time. He has also set eternity in the human heart; yet no one can fathom what God has done from beginning to end (Eccles. 3:1–8, 11 NIV).

―――――――――――――

One of the secrets to a happy life is making sure that when your King David falls it doesn't fall on you. Our faith must not rest in anything other than the certainty of God. It must not depend on symbols or circumstances, accomplishments or past experiences. It must not depend on the blessings of health or wealth or any other good thing. The truth is, bad things will happen to us all. And sooner or later, the King David in your life will fall too. There will be difficult times, times of loss, times that will threaten the strongest of souls. There will be long stretches in your life when you will not hear the voice of God, or you will doubt that what you are hearing is actually His voice.

Like it or not, the New Testament is full of warnings about the unavoidability of stresses and trials, of disappointments and tribulations. In His last conversation with His disciples, Jesus talked at length about the trials that were about to befall them. James actually wrote about trials as a positive thing, suggesting that we should embrace them as an opportunity for growth and strengthening of character. Peter also, almost unbelievably, suggested that we should *rejoice* in the face of trials, rejoice because they are only there to test and refine our faith. Paul addressed the issue extensively in his epistles. The following are just a sample of many passages covering this theme:

"And since we are his children, we are his heirs. In fact, together with Christ we are heirs of God's glory. But if we are to share his glory, we must also share his suffering. Yet what we suffer now is nothing compared to the glory he will reveal to us later" (Rom. 8:17–18 NLT).

"For our present troubles are small and won't last very long. Yet they produce for us a glory that vastly outweighs them and will last forever! … For the things we see now will soon be gone, but the things we cannot see will last forever" (2 Cor. 4:17–18 NLT).

"… I no longer count on my own righteousness through obeying the law; rather, I become righteous through faith in Christ. For God's way of making us right with himself depends on faith. I want to know Christ and experience the mighty power that raised him from the dead. I want to suffer with him, sharing in his death, so that one way or another I will experience the resurrection from the dead!" (Phil. 3:9–11 NLT).

All that being said, I still can't help but ask: Is all this suffering really necessary? Sure, it's inevitable in an imperfect and sinful world, but is it really fair to call it "good"? Why couldn't the good, merciful, tender, forgiving, and gracious God figure out some better way?

That last question is akin to asking a surgeon, "Isn't there an easier way to get rid of my sick appendix than cutting it out?" The hard truth is simply this: suffering is essential on the road to redemption. Jesus proved that point in the extreme. And because of His extreme suffering, we need only experience a relatively "light affliction," as Paul put it. And, yes, affliction and suffering do serve a purpose, the very important purpose of increasing our faith and our capacity to experience the supreme joy of a relationship with God.

In Jesus' last words to His disciples before he was taken to be crucified, He had much to say about the suffering that lay before them. We have already read parts of that passage, which is contained in John, chapters 14–16, where Jesus promised to send the Comforter to His followers. Let's review them again in this context (by the way, the word "Comforter" can also be translated as "Counselor," "Helper," or "Encourager"):

Let not your heart be troubled: ye believe in God, believe also in me. In my Father's house are many mansions: if it were not so, I would have told you. I go to prepare a place for you. And if I go and prepare a place for you, I will come again, and receive you unto myself; that where I am, there ye may be also. ... And I will pray the Father, and he shall give you another Comforter, that he may abide with you for ever; even the Spirit of truth.... I will not leave you comfortless: I will come to you. ... I tell you the truth; It is expedient for you that I go away: for if I go not away, the Comforter will not come unto you; but if I depart, I will send him unto you. ... These things I have spoken unto you, that in me ye might have peace. In the world ye shall have tribulation: but be of good cheer; I have overcome the world (John 14:1–3, 16–18; 16:7, 33 KJV).

Jesus knew His disciples were in for trouble as soon as He left. He anticipated that each one would be threatened by a troubled heart, and He explained the remedy to them. He assured them that what was about to happen was all according to plan. Suffering, trials, and separation were all to be expected, and, through it all, the Spirit of God, the Comforter, the Helper would be right there with them. So Jesus was saying that the remedy for the troubled heart is the Spirit of God. He was also saying that if your heart is troubled, you may have a harder time hearing the voice of His Spirit. It's sort of a paradox. It is both a command and a promise, a symptom and a remedy: "Let not your heart be troubled, neither let it be afraid" (John 14:27 KJV).

---

What kinds of things trouble the human heart? I suppose it's a little different for everyone. But one of the most common worries is about money. Almost everyone worries, sooner or later, about finances, careers, employment, and retirement. Also, most couples will worry about their marriages. And all parents worry about their children. Some of us worry about our health and might genuinely fear the threat of cancer, impairment, or death. It may seem crazy, but many of us worry about these things even if nothing bad actually ever happens.

And then there are the singular tragedies that can happen when we least expect it. The pink slip on your desk notifying you that after twenty years with the company you are now the victim of downsizing. The phone call from the police informing you that your son has been arrested for drunk driving, or your daughter has been in a serious accident. The confession from a spouse that they have been involved in an affair, or that they want a divorce.

Yes, worries and troubles are universal, even in the relative wealth and safety of the modern Western world. So how do we handle these things? Do we turn to God in times of trouble? Do we blame God for our pain? Or do we just try to muddle through?

------

As I reflect now on my life, on the struggles I've had with important decisions, on the ways I've handled the stresses and setbacks, I think I'm beginning to see things a little more clearly. I think I'm beginning to see that, even at those times, God was still very present in my life. I think He may have been speaking to me all along, speaking to me in His third voice, the voice that is felt more than seen or heard. By intention, He remained relatively faint, distant, and veiled. You might say He refused to raise His voice, even when I did not seem to be listening. But, like the good shepherd who went out in the night to find the lost sheep, He never gave up in His pursuit.

There is a story of a time when God spoke to the prophet Elijah that illustrates what I'm talking about. Elijah had just come from Mount Carmel where he had called down fire from heaven and destroyed all the prophets of Baal. It had been an unprecedented victory and a public confirmation of his authority as the representative of God Most High. Yet in the face of all this, Elijah had been struck with fear, fear of the rebellious children of Israel and Queen Jezebel. You could say that Elijah's heart was troubled, and not necessarily for good reasons. He feared for his life and ran off to hide in a cave in the hills. God met him there and the story goes as follows:

Then [Elijah] came there to a cave and lodged there; and behold, the word of the Lord came to him, and He said to him, "What are you doing here, Elijah?"

He said, "I have been very zealous for the Lord, the God of hosts; for the sons of Israel have forsaken Your covenant, torn down Your alters and killed Your prophets with the sword. And I alone am left; and they seek my life, to take it away."

So He said, "Go forth and stand on the mountain before the Lord." And behold, the Lord was passing by! And a great and strong wind was rending the mountains and breaking in pieces the rocks before the Lord; but the Lord was not in the wind. And after the wind an earthquake, but the Lord was not in the earthquake. After the earthquake a fire, but the Lord was not in the fire; and after the fire a sound of a gentle blowing.

When Elijah heard it, he wrapped his face in his mantle and went out and stood in the entrance of the cave. And behold, a voice came to him and said, "What are you doing here, Elijah?" (1 Kings 19:9–13 NASB).

It's not that God can't speak to us in a strong wind or an earthquake or a fire. In fact, He has done all of these things. It's just that He does not always speak in those ways. And I am beginning to believe that they may not be His preferred voice. It may be that God prefers the "sound of gentle blowing," or, as rendered in other versions, a "still small voice." It is a fine line God walks that leaves our freedom of will intact while still assuring us of His presence. A fine line that stimulates our faith while sustaining our hope.

I believe God doesn't want to overwhelm us or force us into submission. Instead, He wants us to use our faith to trust in something that isn't terribly obvious. He knows that the exercise of our faith will grow our souls. And as our souls grow, our capacity to enjoy the company of His presence grows. And in time, as we look back over our lives, we may see more clearly the evidence of His presence. We will then be able to say with the Psalmist, "Surely goodness and mercy shall follow me all the days of my life: and I will dwell in the house of the Lord for ever" (Ps. 23:6 KJV).

# *Epilogue:*
## THE WOMAN AT THE WELL

God revealed the third divine equation, God is spirit, to the most unlikely of characters. She was a Samaritan, a people of mixed race despised by the Jews. And even in her own culture this woman was a social outcast for being openly promiscuous. Yet Jesus chose to reveal to her one of the most profound doctrines in the entire Bible. And isn't that just like God? You see, in His eyes this Samaritan woman was no less worthy of His grace than any of us. Neither was she any more worthy of His wrath. God chose her, possibly to emphasize that point.

The story is told in John, chapter 4. It is sometimes referred to as the story of "the woman at the well," since it was at a well where she and Jesus met. The disciples had left Jesus alone by the well in the heat of the day. They had gone into town for supplies, and while they were away this Samaritan woman came to the well to draw water. Out of the blue, Jesus spoke to her and asked her for some water. The story reads as follows:

> Jesus, tired from the long walk, sat wearily beside the well about noontime. Soon a Samaritan woman came to draw water, and Jesus said to her, "Please give me a drink." He was alone at the time because his disciples had gone into the village to buy some food.

> The woman was surprised, for Jews refused to have anything to do with Samaritans. She said to Jesus, "You are a Jew, and I am a Samaritan woman. Why are you asking me for a drink?"

> Jesus replied, "If you only knew the gift God has for you and who you are speaking to, you would ask me, and I would give you living water."

> "But sir, you don't have a rope or a bucket," she said, "and this well is very deep. Where would you get this living water? And besides, do you think you're greater than our ancestor Jacob, who gave us this well? How can you offer better water than he and his sons and his animals enjoyed?"

> Jesus replied, "Anyone who drinks this water will soon become thirsty again. But those who drink the water I give will never be thirsty again. It becomes a fresh, bubbling spring within them, giving them eternal life."

> "Please, sir," the woman said, "give me this water! Then

I'll never be thirsty again, and I won't have to come here to get water."

"Go and get your husband," Jesus told her.

"I don't have a husband," the woman replied.

Jesus said, "You're right! You don't have a husband—for you have had five husbands, and you aren't even married to the man you're living with now. You certainly spoke the truth!"

"Sir," the woman said, "you must be a prophet. So tell me, why is it that you Jews insist that Jerusalem is the only place of worship, while we Samaritans claim it is here at Mount Gerizim, where our ancestors worshiped?"

Jesus replied, "Believe me, dear woman, the time is coming when it will no longer matter whether you worship the Father on this mountain or in Jerusalem. You Samaritans know very little about the one you worship, while we Jews know all about him, for salvation comes through the Jews. But the time is coming—indeed it's here now—when true worshipers will worship the Father in spirit and in truth. The Father is looking for those who will worship him that way. For God is Spirit, so those who worship him must worship in spirit and in truth" (John 4:6–24 NLT).

This conversation was completely unprecedented. Men of the first century did not talk openly with strange women, and Jews never spoke to Samaritans. The woman naturally bristled. The fact that she continued the conversation demonstrates a remarkable amount of assertiveness and strong will on her part. But Jesus quickly cut through her defenses. Within a matter of minutes, He convinced her that He was a force to be reckoned with. Then gently and deliberately He exposed the nakedness of her heart. She continued to hold her ground and bravely allowed Him to probe more deeply. Perhaps she sensed the true compassion of His nature. For whatever reason, she was rewarded with one of the most profound revelations in all of Scripture: "God is Spirit, so those who worship him must worship in spirit and in truth."

The woman at the well needed to know that God is love. She needed to know that He forgave her and that she would always be precious in His sight. She also needed to know that God is light. She needed to know that He is perfect and holy and that He would make sure that she too became holy. But more than anything else, she needed to know that God is spirit. She needed to know that God could be present with her wherever she was and in every experience of her life. She needed to know that they could have an unbroken relationship.

All her life she had been told that God is not here, that He is up on that mountain or over in Jerusalem. All her life she had been told she was worthless, despicable, and beyond redemption; the god who would have anything to do with her did not exist. All her life she had been looking for a meaningful and secure relationship, only to be abused, neglected, and cast out.

And what if the woman at the well had lived an easy and carefree life? Would she have known the true need of her heart? How would she have responded when Jesus asked for a drink of water? Actually, under other circumstances, she would not even have been at that well in the heat of the day. She would have already filled her jar in the early hours of the morning like all the respectable women of her culture. But, no, she had an appointment with destiny, an appointment that God in His mercy had predetermined, predetermined through a life of pain, doubt, and suffering.

From the very first sin, the sin of Adam and Eve, God knew that the road to redemption must unavoidably be paved with sorrows. In His wisdom, God cursed the woman with pain and sorrow in her relationships with men and her children. In turn, God cursed the man with pain and frustration in his work and his efforts to put food on the table. He did this so that we would never lose sight of our need of Him. Jesus said, "It is not those who are well who need a physician, but those who are sick. I have not come to call the righteous but sinners to repentance" (Luke 5:31–32 NASB). He said this as a rebuke to the self-righteous scribes and Pharisees but also as a promise to those who know their need.

If life has treated you rough and your heart is troubled and you don't know what to do, think about what Jesus offered the woman at the well. Could you use some of that living water in your life? Think also about the experience of the travelers on the road to Emmaus. Their Lord and Messiah had just been executed, and in all likelihood their very lives were forfeited as well. The cause to which they had committed their lives, their fortunes, and their sacred honor had just been destroyed. Yet God Himself came alongside them and warmed them with His presence. He spoke truth, comfort, and peace to their souls. If you are a believer, that same God is standing right beside you now. He knows what you are going through. He knows the decisions you face. He wants you to exercise your faith and listen for Him with the ears of your spirit.

"Let not your heart be troubled, neither let it be afraid" (John 14:27 KJV).

———

The spiritual journey of each man and woman is unique. I have suggested in my story that everyone's journey might have in common a similar process of connecting with the Trinity of God. I have further suggested a correlation between the three Persons of the Trinity (Father, Son, and Holy Spirit), the three Biblical divine equations (God is love, God is light, and God is spirit), and what I have called the three voices of God (words of affirmation, revelation of His nature, and the warmth of His presence.) When crises come into our lives, when our King Davids fall, we are tempted to worry, and the fear that results can threaten the peace and joy God wants us to experience right now. When King David falls in my life it always falls on my connection with the third person of the Trinity. It always makes me doubt the third voice of God, the voice that comes from His Spirit, the voice that says, "I am right here beside you." I believe it happens this way because I am weakest when it comes to understanding relationship, weakest when it comes to "hearing" His presence. Whatever it is that blocks out God's voice for you, and wherever the crises fall, my prayer is that you will see those times as an opportunity to grow in your faith, that you will learn to experience a greater measure of all the aspects of God's wonderful nature, and that you will know increasingly all the fullness of God.

## Appendix

The first time I heard the voice of God

It sounded like music in my ears.

It spoke of mercy and forgiveness.

The first voice answered the question of my soul, **"Who am I?"**

And answered by saying, **"You are my beloved."**

It was the voice of the Father,

The God Who is love.


The second time I heard the voice of God

It shone like a light in my eyes.

It spoke of truth and glory.

The second voice answered the question of my mind, **"Who are You?"**

And answered by saying, **"I am the One Who is holy."**

It was the voice of the Son,

The God Who is light.

Listening a third time to hear the voice of God,

I sense a presence that promises relationship.

A relationship unbroken, transparent, and complete.

The third voice answers the question of my spirit, **"Where are You?"**

And answers by saying, **"I am right here beside you."**

It is the voice of the Spirit,

The God Who is spirit.


The first time I heard God's voice He answered my question, **"Who am I?"** He answered by saying, **"You are my beloved."** His voice sounded like music in my ears. It was the voice of the Father—the God Who is love. It taught me the meaning of mercy and forgiveness.

The second time I heard God's voice He answered my question, **"Who are You?"** He answered by saying, **"I am the One Who** is holy." His voice shone as a light to my eyes. It was the voice of the Son—the God Who is light. It taught me the meaning of holiness and truth.

Today as I listen a third time for God's voice, I am coming to believe that He is answering my question, **"Where are You?"** He is answering by saying, **"I am right here beside you."** This voice feels like a warming presence. It must be the voice of the Spirit—the God Who is spirit. It teaches me the meaning of relationship, transparent and complete.

For more information about

JEFFREY E. HOFFMAN, MD

The Sound of His Voice

please visit:

*www.soundofhisvoice.com*

For more information about

AMBASSADOR INTERNATIONAL

please visit:

*www.ambassador-international.com*

*@AmbassadorIntl*

*www.facebook.com/AmbassadorIntl*